the point of success in Real Estate.

Six most powerful guides.

By

Real estate

Jose Price

All right received

Before the document is duplicated or reproduced in any manner, the publisher's consent must be gained. Therefore, the contents within can neither be stored electronically, transferred, nor kept in a data database. Neither in part nor in full can the document be copied, scanned, faxed, or retained without approval from the publisher or creator.

Table of content

Any estate will benefit from the growing popularity of smart homes, which will only grow in the coming years. The estate will need software that can keep up with their workflows given the increased interest in the property holdings.

Chapter 1

Real Estate smart housing.

Chapter 2

Real Estate environment maintenance/ building renovation…..

Chapter 3

Real EstateStandards for Sustainable Building

Chapter 4

Real Estate avoids errors

Chapter 5

Real estate law of verify, confirm, confirm.

Chapter 6

Real estate beginners' guide

Real estate

Introduction

Any estate will benefit from the growing popularity of smart homes, which will only grow in the coming years. The estate will need software that can keep up with their workflows given the increased interest in the property holdings.

Chapter1

Real Estate smart housing.

What exactly makes a smart estate?

technology

Internet technology is used in "smart buildings" to transform a building's capabilities. Different components of a smart building, such as cameras, sensors, speakers, and heating, automate daily tasks in the house or office. A smart building is designed to maximize tenant productivity while minimizing hardware and facility life-cycle costs by creating a productive workplace.

Despite being more common in commercial real estate, smart features are becoming sought-after additions to homes and apartments for rent and sale. Whether it's by boosting business productivity or connecting a family calendar to security systems, a building that can comprehend how its residents behave is a true game-changer. Estate agents can highlight the advantages that a smart property can provide its tenants by highlighting its features as important selling factors in their sales process. When marketing a property to a potential tenant or buyer, smart technology can make all the difference by providing a more integrated and immersive lifestyle than ordinary structures.

marketing, publicizing, and selling smart commercial or residential properties.

What benefits might clever technology innovation provide for tenants?

It is hardly surprising that many smart buildings today come fully furnished with cutting-edge technology. Smart technology promotes a sense of unity and cohesion in-home technology by automating nearly every element of our daily routines. Smart buildings give their residents a certain kind of ease of life, which makes tenants feel more at home in their spaces. A simple example of this is being able to turn off your bedroom light while in bed using a smartphone app rather than getting out of bed, or families employing smart technology to manage schedules and create reminders. Fundamental design elements in smart building technologies can have a positive impact on how people live in the future. There's no denying that a smart building's greater energy efficiency and lower energy expenses for owners play a significant role in its attraction. smart technology sales great

Smart building technology offers exciting chances for real estate agents to improve the quality of life by enhancing home connectivity. Taking a proactive stance might help real estate brokers sell more houses because buyers are increasingly looking for better property perks.

Any estate will benefit from the growing popularity of smart homes, which will only grow in the coming years. The estate will need software that can keep up with their workflows given the increased interest in the property holdings. Why are smart systems advantageous for infrastructure and real estate in the age of the new normal? smart house technology will significantly increase the quality of buildings and provide quicker infrastructure development times. Building construction no longer takes several years as it did in the past.

Prefabricated units make it feasible to build structures in a matter of days or even a few weeks. Furthermore, the towers are incredibly accurate thanks to positioning technology. By maximizing the utilization of resources, such as land, power, and water, smart cities can increase the safety, security, sustainability, efficiency, and liveability index of metropolitan areas. It makes sense to choose the former whenever possible when using smart systems, even though they can be employed either organically (when creating cities and structures) or inorganically (when renovating existing buildings). Smart cities increase openness and competition in the commercial environment. The emphasis on sustainability and resource efficiency helps to save about 30% of resources, including power, water, and other materials.

"smart tech" in the real estate sector, refers to technology.

cement such as big data and data analytics, AI, robotics, and blockchain. set a new industry standard. However, investing is super coolLeaders in the sector are now actively looking into smart estate Along with investing in real estate-related technological advancement, the sector should review its current value propositions and business strategies. A culture shift, an open innovation approach, and a workforce with new skill sets are all necessary for the full adoption of the smart estate. Real Estate developers and builders, housing organizations, real estate advisors, real estate investors, real estate financiers, and corporations with substantial real estate portfolios make up the property or real estate business. the installation of a smart meter will lower energy usage by increasing tenants' awareness of their usage.

Chapter 2

Real estate

Real Estate environment maintenance/ building renovation…..

Sustainable Building Maintenance: Its Importance for real estate and BeyondSustainability must go beyond building and design as it becomes more crucial to the future of structures and built environments in general. When considering building maintenance, we might take into account Many of the same sustainable ways that may be used for older buildings that may not have been constructed with ecologically friendly ideas at their core, so we don't have to dismiss them when it comes to continuous maintenance of the structures. retrofitting programs, which all demonstrate that sustainability and the environment must be taken into account for the estate's future. In this article, I examine the significance of sustainable building maintenance for all types of structures, including green buildings. Let's first examine the fundamentals of green building and the reasons for its growing significance.

Many of the same sustainable ways may be used for older buildings that may not have been constructed with ecologically friendly ideas at their core, so we don't have to dismiss them when it comes to n continuous maintenance of the structures. retrofitting programs, which all demonstrate that sustainability and the environment must be taken into account for the estate's future.

In this article, I examine the significance of sustainable building maintenance for all types of structures, including green buildings. Let's first examine the fundamentals of green building and the reasons for its growing significance. concepts can be applied to every step of the construction process, from planning to construction to use and maintenance. The green building considers the effects on the environment as well as preserving and safeguarding the neighborhood. Buildings can be made to use less energy, and a variety of structures have the potential to be more environmentally friendly. There is discussion over whether green buildings are more expensive and raise prices, but in actuality, they should save overall building costs and enhance energy efficiency.

Benefits of a good maintenance system.

Real estate

lowering waste

using technologies and renewable energy sources

lowering the wastewater

Using morally-sound materials

attempting to lessen pollution

providing users of the building with cleaner and safer working environments

enhanced air quality

constructing and maintaining with ecologically friendly, sustainable techniques

Financial Advantages.

however, provide several financial advantages, particularly in the area of lower operational expenses, particularly lower energy bills, waste, and water rates. sustainability and environmental preservation, which continues into maintenance as well as design and construction.Maintaining a building benefits everyone who uses it, not just the tenants. To maintain the value of their properties when they are put up for sale, building owners keep their assets in good working condition. The type of facility will determine whether a "jack of all trades" or numerous personnel with varying payroll expertise are required.

Building Upkeep TypesThere is three main categories of building maintenance.

These are scheduled preventative maintenance techniques that guard a facility against wear and tear and keep it functional. The frequency of routine maintenance tasks can be set to be performed daily, weekly, or intermittently. These tasks include sweeping, removing debris, lubricating hinges, inspecting utility systems, and repainting.

The structural integrity of a structure is maintained and damage is avoided through preventive maintenance procedures. They make the structure more qualified.

Repair and Maintenance

These are steps made to make a building more practical and comfortable. Managers must have a corrective maintenance program in place because it is impossible to completely prevent damage or decay. As fast as possible, everything is returned to functioning condition thanks to corrective maintenance.

Building Maintenance Job Categories

Different maintenance tasks require different specializations. Workers fall into a variety of groups based on their expertise and job responsibilities.

Through a well-established maintenance organization or facilities management, various building sectors now maintain their buildings. that offer avenues for the current issues and challenges impeding sustainable and efficient maintenance practices, even though earlier studies have identified the current issues of building maintenance practices and their effects. The scarcity of studies to date has led to evidence from the literature calling for additional study that offers systemic ways to enhance sustainable and effective practices

By offering systematic techniques for efficient and sustainable building maintenance procedures, this book aims to close this gap. It may also be seen as a response to earlier research as well as the growing concerns of governments and academics regarding the sustainability of buildings, answering the present requirement by proposing strategic techniques that can enhance sustainable building performance.

Chapter 3

Real Estate Standards for Sustainable Building

Standards for Sustainable Building Contracts and Procurement

To ensure that all ethical focuses are the same and can be followed, the procurement process is becoming more personable and enabling a deeper knowledge of all parties. As long-term strategies are properly planned out and sustainable and environmentally-led maintenance plans can be put in place to prevent all the real estate works from being undone, a closer and more consultative connection between and with contractors can help. Building consultants, other parties participating in the design and construction of the building, and the building owner can express their commitment to sustainable practices and guarantee that the sustainability measures are upheld throughout.

A better grasp of the maintenance needed throughout real estate life can also be ensured by having a clearer understanding of the building's machinery and equipment. Thanks to planning and an understanding of the building's requirements as it ages, a sustainable approach to all future maintenance can be emphasized and costings may be planned as effectively as possible, with no unpleasant surprises or significant hidden expenses in the future.

Engineering and Surveying Knowledge for Sustainable Building Upkeep

Numerous professionals are needed during the planning, design, and construction of a building, but they don't frequently need to collaborate or overlap. Engineers and surveyors are examples of this. However, if they cooperate, it can lessen resource waste and wasteful spending throughout the process. To reduce equipment waste, and access time, and anticipate issues early in the process, the two processes can operate simultaneously. This will help you avoid wasting money and time on unneeded future repairs or replacements.

An engineer visiting the building to install equipment on the roof would be an example. It would be logical to utilize this period to allow surveyors to evaluate and examine the roof area and recommend any work that may need to be done concurrently. Additionally, it may be able to use the same access solutions and expedite any necessary repairs that might not have been identified until a later time. This prevents further inconvenience. Even while more work may not always be required, being extra cautious is advantageous if it results in long-term cost savings.

Keeping Building Services and Performance Sustainable

Sustainability extends beyond a building's framework and aesthetic. More than energy badges, performance reports, and proof of due diligence will be desired by building occupants. Their attention will also be on how a room will function for its occupants or users and whether they can comfortably use the space. A building's functionality does decline over time, so it is particularly crucial to think about long-term and reactive maintenance strategies to guarantee the building can always provide the best performance for all of its users.

This implies that a consistent and high-quality level of communication must be maintained between the owners of the estate, the professionals who perform maintenance services, and the building's users, who typically take the shape of facility managers or others. While some maintenance chores may have deadlines, others may rely on the building's condition following an inspection and assessment. For the building's health, communication and a flexible attitude toward environmentally friendly management techniques are essential.

It's time to embrace real estate as the way of the future.

Real estate

Although requirements are driving the transition to real estate and more sustainable construction and maintenance, it also has an ethical and moral component. Businesses that demonstrate their dedication to a cause, including using smart building and sustainable practices, are more likely to attract customers. Building owners and architects can take inspiration from structures like the Building in London and the Transbay Tower in San Francisco that were built with sustainability.

Real estate is the industry benchmark for environmental management and outlines the requirements for a successful environmental management system.

Building Transformation develops sustainable building maintenance strategies to expertly repair and maintain structures so they last. To set up a sustainable solution that satisfies the requirements of 21st-century buildings and global sustainability goals, pay attention to this book.

Highly skilled personnel are needed to enable safe and suitable entry to buildings with particularly difficult-to-reach regions so that the right level of care or maintenance may be carried out.

Many variables will affect the access services that are appropriate for your facility. Considerable factors include:

• The building's age and historical value; • Any rules, such as listing requirements, that you need to be aware of

Building height and locations that are difficult to access

Modern scaffolding is adaptable and customizable, and it offers a secure platform for workers at heights, enhancing safety. It is simpler to erect quickly in a variety of settings, including buildings of various shapes and sizes.

• Because it has a flat surface, the scaffolding gives the employees a secure foothold. It facilitates workers' ability to balance in various positions.

• Scaffolds are frequently employed to offer access for historic building inspection, upkeep, and repair.

• When compared to scaffolding, which can take a lot of time to erect, modify, and disassemble, setup takes less time and costs less money.

• Rope equipment is lighter and easier to erect and take down than scaffolding, allowing for speedier access.

• One of the least invasive and dangerous access choices when it comes to a building's façade.The laws around employing rope access systems are strict, there is no additional terrain, flat or otherwise, to work from, and this means work can start right away. There was just one case of mortality documented when using rope access equipment.

• Offers a risk-free method for working at heights. Safety precautions are taken into account in every project due to regulations surrounding working at heights.

For an asset's value to be maintained, sustainable building upkeep is essential. By managing operations cost-effectively, it keeps building systems operating properly, increases the lifespan of equipment, and maintains indoor comfort in structures. Maintenance delivers sustainability and a higher return on investment with a building management system.

Maintenance Methods

To develop a comprehensive building maintenance strategy, several forms of maintenance are required. These consist of:

Repairing broken things is a form of corrective maintenance.

routine scheduled or planned maintenance, such as changing the air filter in a heating, ventilation, and air conditioning system according to the suggested timetable.

preventive maintenance, such as fixing leaky roofs, is done to keep equipment in working order or extend its lifespan. The data-driven preventative maintenance paradigm, however, is where smart building technologies shine.

Creating Sustainable Maintenance Practices with Big Data

Building systems may be precisely managed and optimized at any moment with modern smart technology. This is accomplished by integrating analytics into preventative maintenance techniques

An advanced analytics platform finds anomalies and inefficiencies and suggests remedies by continuously gathering, sorting and analyzing data from all connected systems. Additionally, it makes advantage of machine learning to forecast performance. Facilities managers may easily manage systems with these insights by making small adjustments to optimize as necessary, then scaling up sustainable maintenance procedures as more data becomes available over time.

Removing Seasonal Maintenance

Seasonal maintenance has traditionally been a key component of building upkeep. These schedules, however, were simply based on an educated assumption as to when problems would occur. If a problem arose after hours, it might not be discovered until it was severe and would need expensive repairs.

Intelligent systems alter this.

Data-driven maintenance eliminates the need for arbitrary, timing-based intervention. Building equipment's data output provides excellent visibility into how that equipment is operating, negating the need for physical examination and pointless intervention. You can save money by not spending resources maintaining equipment that is currently in excellent operating condition by using a system that only warns you when problems arise. Additionally, you acquire the capacity to respond to problems as soon as they emerge, long before they result in catastrophic equipment failure, unanticipated costs, or occupant complaints.

Traditional Maintenance Plans Must Go

The conventional maintenance programs that service providers offer are interval-based, and the suggested intervals are very short. Callouts outside of this window are billed as emergencies and will undoubtedly be more expensive. Reliance on such plans is eliminated by putting in place data-driven, sustainable maintenance methods. It is now possible to only undertake maintenance when it is truly necessary and at a more predictable cost.

The interaction between building owners, facilities managers, and service providers is fundamentally altered as a result. Real knowledge of how your building operates gives you the power to choose wisely between service agreements and better control expenditures. To make sure you are accomplishing your sustainability goals and getting the most for your money, you may also validate changes based on objective data.

Chapter 4

Real Estate avoids errors

The goal is to get to a fair agreement. Avoid paying too much for the house. There are many fantastic investment homes available, so resist the urge to purchase the first house you come across. This tactic assists you in depending less on variables outside your control, such as market growth or the state of the economy. Real estate purchases at negotiated prices are followed by the creation of additional value through intelligent management, suitable upgrades, and renovations, a strong operations plan, and a capable workforce.

Having reliable exit strategies for investments

Refinance the home, withdraw some cash, and put the money earned into more real estate. Give the property a new purposeYou can better see how you will run the property today if you have a sound investment exit strategy.

Decide on the kind of diversification you want in your portfolio. For instance, you might choose the following as your diversity goal:

Flipping real estate quickly.

Rental homes with a long-term lease.

Strong portfolio diversification will shield you from each asset class's brief volatility.

Create short- and long-term investment plans that cover cash flow, passive income, equity growth, and capitalization (how you take money out of your investments).

Your liquidity requirements are another crucial factor to take into account here. You don't want to be in a position where you desperately need money but it's locked up for a while.

Choose Active or Passive Investing as Your Style

Do you require a sense of ownership over your investments? How much time do you have to handle your portfolio actively?

Through experience, I've been able to strike a decent balance and have come to terms with what I enjoy doing. When I first started investing in real estate, I focused on single-family homes but soon realized that the hands-on management required consumed too much of my time. Later, I relocated to multifamily homes and apartment complexes that supported contracting a professional management firm from a third party.

By altering my investment strategy, I was able to free up more time to focus on business development, asset acquisition, and asset management rather than daily property maintenance.

Make no errors Never invest simply because others are doing it.

This law is self-evident. It is simple to get caught up in the fallacy that anything everyone does must be beneficial. The risk here is that if you think the crowd or organization has already done it, you are less likely to conduct your research.

One of the most well-liked methods for breaking into the real estate market is house flipping. The act of purchasing, renovating, and then reselling a home to make money is known in real estate as flipping.

Prehabbing: Prehabbing is the process of preparing a home for sale by making a few small cosmetic improvements. The investor buying the house will frequently then fully renovate it.

Some local investors, who entered the condominium conversion industry too late, are renting out residential units of condominium quality as apartments. You do not want to make such an expensive error.

Landscape design: If you can't make visitors enjoy the outside of your property, they're not going to be interested in spending the time to go inside. Contrary to popular belief, curb appeal has a big impact on real estate prices and costs very little.

Painting: For novices looking to improve the appearance of a property, painting offers a minimally expensive option.

Real estate

Chapter 5

Real estate law of verify, confirm, confirm.

Always do your due diligence and thoroughly review all of your financial records, books, reports, data, and physical assets. Get everything down on paper. Speak with individuals who have expertise in a specific asset class and contrast the figures. Request references, then make contact with those people.

Make sure you believe the numbers make sense by running them. Get a member of your team to run the figures for you if you lack confidence in your ability to do so, and ask them to give you their assessment of the offer. possess the required tools and expertise with their use (or have a team that does). These resources will contain spreadsheets for financial analysis and due diligence on commercial real estate investments, among others.

You must have a thorough understanding of the tax implications and benefits (on your investment as well as your present income) before investing. When investing, consider the tax consequences for the current year, the following years, and the day you sell your investment.

A strong team is essential.

Consider buying and selling real estate as a business. Your responsibility is to manage the resources of your business and implement plans to expand your investment holdings. When you're always performing minor repairs or micromanaging your property, that's difficult to do.

You don't want to impair your ability to regularly carry out your objectives or lose sight of your long-term goals.

Never forget that only you are the expert on your investment psychology, objectives, priorities, risk tolerance, and other factors.

It might be beneficial and enjoyable to keep a record of your financial guidelines. You can steer clear of executing agreements you're not completely confident about by following real estate investing regulations. You can start setting down your financial guidelines.

The idea of assembling a fantastic team can easily overwhelm new investors. Don't worry. You are not required to conduct interviews, post job openings on Craig's List, or hire someone. By networking, you may assemble a fantastic team.

Just like investing directly in real estate, financing real estate transactions can be risky and speculative. Before making a choice, always do your research. Investors may choose to take part in a single project or a portfolio of projects, and they will be paid out either monthly or quarterly. Furthermore, it's a great way to geographically diversify your real estate holdings. When using a real estate platform, investors must pay platform membership fees, and the money may be illiquid and subject to lockup periods.

Chapter 6

Real estate beginners' guide

Real estate investment may be scary, especially if you are new to it. It can be difficult to know where to begin, how much money to put up, and what to look for in a property before you buy it. You may feel as though you are constantly observing individuals who appear to have it all together when it comes to real estate investment, house flipping, wholesaling, or managing rentals. How do they all understand how to operate in this field of real estate investing? We recognize that even though the real estate investors you see today may appear to have it all together, they too had to go through a period of learning and undoubtedly made some mistakes before arriving at where we are now. To help you learn more about how to start investing in real estate successfully right away, we have listed the basic habits of successful real estate investors.

Recognize the Market

If you want to be successful when you start investing in real estate, you must first and foremost understand the market. Knowing the market will give you an advantage because you'll know what houses are selling for, how much you should be paying, and what you could also get for them if you decide to sell.

Recognize the Risks Associated

If you've already decided to engage in real estate investing, you probably already know that there will be risk involved. However, knowing the risk associated with investments will be the next realization for all successful real estate investors. Knowing the risks involved will enable you to determine how much you are genuinely willing to commit given the level of risk involved.

investing in real estate

Be persistent

It can be challenging to maintain patience, especially when engaging in the thrilling process of buying a new piece of property. When you are waiting for the ideal chance to arise, patience will be crucial. Avoid buying the first property that crosses your path; doing so is a surefire way to lose money. Instead, wait patiently for the ideal chance to come along.

Do business based on facts, not feelings

Being able to keep emotions out of your real estate business is another easy habit of successful real estate. Successful investors focus their purchases and investments on data and market expertise, not on feelings or hopes.

Plan ahead

Making a plan is crucial for any real estate investor to succeed. Make a plan for the property as soon as you possess a piece of land, a structure, a home, or any other real estate-related object. What will you add, what will you take away, and what will you change?

Stay Informed

A key factor in a real estate investor's success is continuing their education. This entails remaining informed about market shifts and trends as well as anything else that has an impact on the home or real estate industry. You will keep moving forward in your success as long as you keep learning.

Be Honest and Uphold High Principles

Your success in real estate investing is greatly influenced by your honesty and morality. Building trust in your professional and business circles will have a positive ripple effect across your entire company, resulting in success for your overall investment enterprise. You are more likely to have strong, profitable sales and month-to-month renters the more potential tenants and buyers trust you. Good tenants and sales spill over into your recommendations.

Promote referrals

Real estate investors who are successful encourage word-of-mouth. Referrals are a good way for the friends and relatives of any real estate investor's prior or present clients to learn that they, too, can have a positive experience with you. generating more companies for you!

Real estate

Find Assistance, But Remain Active

Finding assistance is another approach to increasing the success of your real estate ventures. If your real estate investing efforts are somewhat successful, you may ultimately reach a point where you'll need assistance managing your properties. Find assistance; doing so will enable you to maintain control of the property and maximize the use of your real estate. Getting assistance does not imply becoming disengaged, however; it is advantageous to be active so that you can monitor the progress of your investments and make necessary changes and adjustments.

Create A Network

Establishing a network will help your business succeed. While it will take some time as you start to establish yourself and your investments, it will eventually give you possibilities for your firm to expand and adapt in ways that will continue to support its success.

Consider investments to be businesses

A wise investor will take the time to carefully consider the costs, labor, and profits to make sure that your net income is positive on every investment, whether it be a rental property, a home renovation, or anything else.

Put Efficiency First

The key to being a successful investor is to make more money than you spend. The more effectively you can manage your properties, work on your real estate, or make any modifications, updates, or repairs, the more likely you are to boost your revenue.

Maintain (reasonable) Partner Happiness

Keeping your partner happy is the last easy habit we have for you today from a successful real estate investor. If you are an investor, you may have partnered with someone else to raise additional funds. A successful business and investment activity must be handled by you and your partner in harmony. While we are not advising you to comply with every request made by your spouse, be sure to meet in the middle and express your gratitude for their confidence in you.

Commence networking

The best method to broaden your horizons is by networking, especially if you're starting a real estate investing firm. You will: through networking

Meet other prosperous real estate investors (mentors) and learn from them.

Identify new markets

Utilize recommendations to find new service providers and contractors

forward with your education

Find investment opportunities that the general public cannot access.

Whom do your acquaintances and pals know? You can probably find successful investors by making a few phone calls and asking for warm introductions. Never undervalue the importance of expanding your network.

partners content.

Doesn't this nearly seem like a no-brainer? If you work with partners on your deals, you are aware of the need to satisfy them. Right?

There's a delicate line between content investors and those that want to manage your company for you, though. Having investment partners with no prior knowledge of real estate investing is not uncommon.

Define your partnership structure out front. As an illustration, in the initial phases of the investment process:

Try not to forecast the top or bottom of a real estate market. When you become aware of a market movement, the majority of that movement has already occurred. Whatever the temptation, avoid putting all of your money into one "hot" asset class and avoid diversification altogether.

Don't put more money into investments than you can afford to lose comfortably.

Understand your worst-case scenarios and decide if you can survive them. Take calculated chances. Make sure you have the money for the maintenance of your real estate investments as well as an emergency reserve.

The three most crucial team members are your commercial broker, real estate mentor, and property management business. These three crucial people provided me with the majority of my recommendations for potential team members.

Characteristics of Succeeding Real Estate Investors

It is simple to start doubting your abilities as a first-time real estate investor and to question whether you have what it takes to be successful. None of life's success stories, though, start flawlessly. The most crucial trait for an investor is temperament, not intelligence, according to real estate tycoon Warren Buffett. Learning from mistakes and continually reinventing yourself is both doable. You can begin to emulate some of the following characteristics of prosperous real estate investors right away:

Passionate

Self-disciplined

Driven

Imaginative

Bold

Principled

Flexible

Economical

Team-oriented

Personable

Real estate

You're not the only one if you're unsure about where to begin. Achieving your financial objectives through real estate investing is a terrific idea, but it can be challenging for a beginner to understand the steps involved. We provide pointers, counsel, beginner-friendly tactics, jargon, and blunders to avoid addressing this. This real estate investing handbook is one you should treasure.

How Does Investing in Real Estate Produce Profits?

A tried-and-true way to gain money is through real estate investing, and there are many different ways to do it. Value appreciation and rental income are the two primary strategies:

Property values have risen over the years all across history. This rise in value appreciation is what we refer to. Location is the most important factor to base your investment on, according to any expert. The perceived attractiveness of an area increases along with property values. Have you heard the saying, "Buy the worst-looking house in the best neighborhood?" Some of this is accurate. Purchasing a home you can renovate in a desirable area is preferable to purchasing a mediocre home in an undesirable one. Investing in a developing

Real estate

area is another option.

www.ingramcontent.com/pod-product-compliance
Lightning Source LLC
Chambersburg PA
CBHW070614220526
45467CB00003B/1421